Lipstick on His Forehead
and Tears in His Fur

Adventures of a Therapy Dog

Oh, what a ride we had!

DJ CLANCY

authorHOUSE®

AuthorHouse™
1663 Liberty Drive
Bloomington, IN 47403
www.authorhouse.com
Phone: 1-800-839-8640

Published by AuthorHouse   03/28/2012

ISBN: 978-1-4685-7507-1 (sc)
ISBN: 978-1-4685-7506-4 (e)

Library of Congress Control Number: 2012905816

Contents

Brady O'Shea Clancy
05-12-2000 to 03-31-2011
Oh, what a ride we had!

When I first saw you, I tried not to look.
But seeing those brown eyes, that's all it took.
I fell in love with a sweet, gentle puppy that would melt the hearts of many.
No matter where we went, people loved you, and there were plenty.
I knew from the start, you had a special gift.
How to share your soul—that was my quest.
You became my partner in a task so very special.
The love you gave people was unconditional!
I knew the time would come when you would get older.
But it was so hard to see you getting slower.
The time has come to say our good-byes, with one last look in your gentle eyes.
That afternoon, when I was so sad,
A butterfly came by, and on his wings, a message he had.
"Don't be sad, Mommy. I'm okay."
We always could talk in our own special way.
The rainbow I saw that day after rain,
I knew it was you, and it helped ease the pain.
You are missed and loved by many, a comfort to me,
And someday it will again be you and me.
Oh, what a ride we had!

Love, Mommy

Acknowledgements

Thank you to my family and friends who encouraged me to write down my memories. Your support gave me the strength to share my feelings and to cope with my loss.

A special thank you to Evie Sullivan for dotting my i's and crossing my t's. You always have my back.

To Ann Wirtz, from Wirtz Design Studio, thank you for organizing my work to fruition. With your help, my book became a reality in print.

My love and appreciation to the Day family for trusting me to raise your puppy, Brady. The joy he gave Gary and I will remain in our hearts forever.

My sweet Brady, I know in my heart that you helped me find the words to share our story. I felt your presence with me every step of the way; thank you. I love you and miss you.

Prologue

I had a dog once before, a dog named Barnaby. He was a wonderful golden whom I loved deeply, but my main focus at that time was my family. Helping in our family business, raising our two children, and of course, being involved with lots of their school activities kept me very busy. When I lost him, I was devastated. The pain was so great that I never wanted another dog. Barnaby had found me, but I didn't open my mind and heart to him to realize he was my soul mate from many lifetimes ago. I didn't really listen to him, which I will always regret. I know now he understood; that's why he came back to find me again, so he could have another chance to train *me*.

Six years went by, during which our business went through tough times but survived, kids graduated college, and I was busy planning our daughter's wedding. Another dog was the furthest thing from my mind. One afternoon a neighbor called, saying that there was a litter of new puppies on our street; they were golden retrievers that I had to see. Well, I said, "No, I don't." The last thing I needed was a puppy, with the wedding less than two months away.

"Just look," she said, and she was relentless.

"Okay, okay," I replied. That decision changed my life. This little guy, with those deep brown eyes, just melted my heart. Little did I know that I would fall in love so completely and experience incredible events that many people only dream of. He had found me, and this time he got through to me; we were to be a team. Slowly I realized that this was not just an ordinary dog; this one had a gift, and he wanted me to help him on his journey of healing—not medical miracles but the healing of hearts.

If He Could Talk

My name is Brady O'Shea Clancy, and I'm a golden retriever puppy. I've been in this position before, being reborn, I mean. I was a horse once, but I didn't meet enough people, and I had to stand around a lot. Oh, my aching back! I tried being a cat before, but lots of people didn't like cats. I really didn't like chasing after mice and eating birds; too much effort, and for what? Food was given to me every day, so why bother? Plus, I have a very sensitive stomach, you know, especially to feathers. In addition, I had to constantly clean my fur, which drove me crazy, not to mention the hairballs. So I decided to be a dog again. Everyone loves a dog, right? I had to go through all the puppy stuff that I had forgotten because I wanted to come back to be with my soul mate. I'd had a great life as Barnaby, but she didn't know who I really was. I was with her for ten years when my body gave out and I had to leave. I wanted to come back into her life right away, but she was too heartbroken to love again. I had to wait.

I will come back, I promise, and then you'll realize who I am. I had to wait six years.

Brady was not always my name. When I was born, the human family I lived with called me Tony. I have two brothers and two sisters.

When we played too rough, our mom would roll us over on our backs, bite our necks, and growl at us to stop. But of course, a little later we'd rough it up again. The humans we lived with were cool—for humans—but they spoke a funny language that I couldn't understand. So we all just ran around getting into mischief as the humans tried to corral us, but it was a hopeless cause. Lots of humans started coming over to see us. Let's run! Where's the ball, where's the ball? Oh, she has it in her hand. Wait, don't throw it. I want it. Why'd she do that? She's pointing at the ball. Yeah, I see where it is. What? You want me to get it? But you threw it away! Oh, all right, I guess I'll run over and get it. Now what? You want it back? Oh, now I remember, I get it! This is a game humans like to play with dogs. All right then, I can learn to like this, especially when my sister Tina gets to the ball first. She brings it to me to play, but I run away with it to the human, and I get the pat on the head. This works for me.

One day, a human came over to pick up my sister Tina. They took her outside into what looked like a big monster that made a lot of noise. They all went inside this monster, and they went away. Where's Tina? Where is she? Did the monster eat her? My humans were saying something very softly; they seemed happy. Maybe Tina went on a new adventure. Maybe I can go too someday. Then other humans came over to take Wilber and Kobe away. Where are they all going? At least Daphne is still here. I'm eight weeks old now, trying to understand a little more of this strange human world. I met a big dog the other day who said I'd have to go to a new family soon. Then he said they would probably give me a new name too. Why? Tony is kind of cool, isn't it? Is that where Tina, Wilber, and Kobe went?

I was playing in the front yard one day when I saw her! She was my mommy from years ago. Somehow she had found me. I have forgotten a lot in the last six years, and things have changed, but I knew we'd find each other again. I just need to convince her of who I am. I tried to tell her when my name was Barnaby, but she didn't hear me. She's the one I was looking for, I'm positive. Here she comes. Take me, take me. You're supposed to take me. Wait, don't go! Where's she going? I can feel that she wants me, but she's afraid of something. Is she afraid to love me? I still love her!

The next day, she comes back with a male human. It's Daddy from before! They play with me and roll around on the grass. I don't think they know who I really am yet, but I know they want me. The humans talk and, wait a minute, Mommy is crying while saying good-bye to me. No, no. I want to go with you. Don't leave me! My human family is talking to each other as if they are trying to decide on something. I'm supposed to go to someone else? Please, no. I have to get through to them somehow. I want to be with Mommy and Daddy again. Why can't you hear me? I'm so sad, I don't even want to play with Mom or Daphne.

A few days pass, but Mommy doesn't come back. My birth mom doesn't want to play much anymore; she said she doesn't feel well. Maybe all of us puppies just wore her out. Kobe, Tina, and Wilber are gone, and now I lost Mommy and Daddy too.

My human mom is talking to me while putting something around my neck. I'm not going in the monster that Tina went in. No way. Wait. She and Dad are carrying me as we go down the street. Wonder why? We're walking up to a house that looks familiar. When the door opens, I look and start twisting, wiggling until my mom puts me down. I run to the humans in the doorway. It's Mommy and Daddy! They brought me home. She's crying but laughing at the same time. I think she's happy. She picks me up, hugs and kisses me; still crying, she hugs my human birth mom too. My face is all wet. I don't know why and I don't care. I'm with Mommy. She keeps saying the same words to me: "I love you!" Now this is where I'm supposed to be.

Come on, let's explore! Is this my bed? Wait a minute, it's in a cage? You don't really think I'm going to go in there, do you? I'll just go in there, get what looks like a new toy for me, and get out. Here we go. Got it! All right, let's play. Mom is pointing to herself, saying the word *Mommy*. Well, I already know that, so I just tilt my head and play cute. Then she points to me and says B-r-a-d-y. Brady, that's my new name, just like the big dog said. She is pointing to her mate, saying *Daddy*. Another cute tilt of my head was all I had to do to get a kiss on my forehead. I wonder if they can see that I am smiling too, because I know this house. I love to explore places, and oh, those smells. I've missed those smells! Some more humans came over to meet me. Everybody loves me. I had a little accident in the house, but she didn't get mad. I guess I was too excited, so she carried me outside to the grass. Now I remember—I'm supposed to pee in the grass.

The Cat

What was that noise? A high-pitched *what?* Hissing and spitting. My brothers didn't do that.

Mom said, "This is Samantha, our cat." *A cat?* Oh well, I'm sure she'll love me too. I'm the new cute kid, remember? Everybody loves me. Hey there . . . how you doing? "Meow!" Hey! What'd you hit me for? That hurt! I think I'm bleeding. Am I bleeding? What's with your teeth and those nails?

She said, "Leave me alone, buster. *I own this house,* and don't you forget it."

What's her problem? Oh well. Come on Mom, let's play. People come for a celebration of some sort, and I'm the center of attention because I'm the new kid. I'm tired. I think I'll sleep for a while. There is a small bed here so I think I'll . . .

"Oh no you don't. That's *my* bed!" It's that *cat* again. Okay, okay, just don't hit me. One of these days cat, I'll win you over. You'll love me; just wait and see.

One day I end up at my birth family's house again. Did Mommy change her mind and doesn't want me after all? My dog mom is there, but she doesn't seem to care, not even getting up from her bed. The next morning, they take my dog mom away in that monster. They come back alone, so sad, crying all the time. Where is my Mom? What happened? Did the monster eat her too?

That afternoon, Mommy does come back to get me. She didn't leave me after all! There was a wedding, and I was too young to be left alone for a long time. She is so happy to see me, but all of a sudden, she is sad too. Turns out that my birth mom died; she was very sick. I really don't understand, but I feel that everyone is sad, so I'm sad too.

Home at last, where I belong.

I'll just lie here in the middle of the floor. Mom picks me up to put me in another bed. I guess this is mine. I smell something really good. Who said dinner? Yum . . . I'm hungry. The days go on, and I'm learning the human talk more every day. Mom says we're going for a ride. She's carrying me to that monster! No way! Mom says it's okay, that she'll be with me, but I don't know about this. She lets me sit in the back as she starts the noise. She says this is a car, and we'll go to lots of fun places. I'm nervous, but I trust her, so here we go. I just hope I don't pee on the back seat. This isn't too bad. It turns out riding in the car is one of my favorite things to do, because I'm able to go to lots of places. The best part is that I don't have to share Mom with that crazy, mean, sixteen-pound *cat*.

Mom said it's time for dinner. The cat's getting some too, but she's up on the table, and hers smells a lot better than mine. What's up with that? Just let me smell her food. Maybe if she's not looking, I can get a quick bite. Oh no, here comes that long paw again with those sharp nails swiping down at me! This has to stop. Who does she think she is? She heard me.

"I'm the cat, I rule!" she hissed back. Someday I'll show that cat. She looks at me and raises her tail, as if to say, *we'll see about that,* as she leaves the room. We go upstairs, where I have a nice big bed next to Mom and Dad. It is so much better sleeping in their room, even with Samantha here too. I didn't want to sleep in that cage all alone downstairs.

A new day. Hooray! I have to get down these stairs first. Whoops, I missed the last step. Come on, Mom, I'm going to get to the back door first. I am beginning to understand more and more of the human language.

Mommy takes me outside the house for what she calls "a walk." But what is this thing around my neck? It's attached to a rope of some kind that she is holding, so I have to go wherever Mom wants to go. Wait a minute—I want to go over there, not here. "I have to keep you safe, so you have to wear a collar, and this is a leash to lead you in the right direction," said Mom.

Okay for now, I thought. Going for walks was fun. We'd meet lots of people, and everybody loves me. Remember, I'm the new kid. But the best part of a walk is that the cat isn't coming. I made a new friend who looks just like me, only bigger. She's called Rusty. "Hey, dude, how's it going?" she said. "So you're the new kid. I heard you have a pink forehead. What's up with that?"

I looked at Mom. Somehow she knew, so she started rubbing my forehead like I had dirt on it or something. I didn't know why, but okay. When we went on walks, we always had to go her way. Well, maybe I can make a game of this situation. Let's see, I can't use my paws, but I can use my mouth. Let's play tug-of-war. I'll bite the leash, and you pull on it. Yeah. This will be fun! "Not so fast," Mommy said. "This is not a pleasant walk, and I will not be pulled down the street."

Being reborn is the pits. I have to put up with all this discipline and I have to learn all this stuff again. "Where's your sense of humor, Mom?"

She stopped, with a strange expression on her face as if she heard me. Did she hear me? I think she did! Wait, wait, what are you doing? Next thing I know, I'm on the ground, on my back with Mommy biting my neck. I think she had enough of my nonsense. My dog mom did the same to me when I got too rough and wouldn't listen. Okay, okay, I get it!

I Say This Way, and You Say That Way

Brady is getting older, so now it's time for real leash training. We had a trainer come to the house to teach us how to train him. We had to learn to be the alpha. Of course, Brady wanted to be the alpha too, which did create a problem. He always wanted to go the opposite way I wanted to go. He must smell an adventure calling; a dog thing, I'm sure. Practice makes perfect, so practice we did. We walked all over, but every time we met someone or saw another dog, all he wanted to do was to say hello as all the discipline went out the window. So, more practice was needed.

I think he's got it. "This is going quite well, Brady. Let's try practicing some off-leash walking to see how you do," I said. He did pretty well, staying right by my side until we came to a house that had the front door open. Well, off he went, running right into the house with me running after him, trying to remember the commands I had been taught. Yelling after him, I said, "Stop, wait, here, come, oh d—!" I found him with a little girl and her dad, with smiles on everyone including Brady. He had charmed them too. I apologized, took my dog—on leash—and home we went. Back to square one.

The hardest training was walking on the breakwater with many people close together with lots of dogs. When someone came by us, he always got in front of them till they stopped to pet him. Most people did, and they were very nice. But one man who had a dog didn't want to meet Brady, and his dog bit Brady's nose. I was furious because the man didn't care that his dog drew blood; he just walked off. Brady and I were in shock, when a thought came to me: *I can't believe he didn't like me.*

"Brady, was that you?" I asked. It must have been what I was thinking, right? After that, Brady was actually more careful not to always get into a person or a dog's face.

He mastered walking on lead as we enjoyed our walks, plus he knew where every avocado tree was in the neighborhood. One windy day, we were on our usual morning walk when he pulled me toward one of the trees. I'm not sure if he remembered that the last time it was so windy, there were lots of avocados on the ground. Maybe he smelled them; I don't know, another dog thing. Sure enough, there must have been a dozen on the grass. He didn't know which one to pick up first. He had one in his mouth while trying to pick up another, but then the first one fell out. He tried repeatedly, but it couldn't be done. He finally settled on me carrying one while he carried another, but of course, we would have to go right home to eat a piece of that jackpot find. For the next three days, all he wanted to do was walk by that same avocado tree. He knew the way, and I could see that he was hoping for another jackpot. But, as so often happens in Las Vegas, you only hit the jackpot once, if you're lucky. The avocados where gone. Being very disappointed, he hung his head when he couldn't find any. We were about to leave, when an avocado fell from that tree, landing right in front of his nose. I couldn't believe it. *He* couldn't believe it. I even looked up into the tree to see if someone had been picking them and saw his disappointment, but no one seemed to be there. A thought came to me: *I knew I'd find one!* I looked at him with the avocado already in his mouth. "Brady?" I said.

He loved to go to the park, where there was an off-leash area. He made lots of friends as he played with other dogs. We walked around the park off leash, enjoying nature, when up went his nose. It must have been a rabbit, as he ran up the hill, once again ignoring my commands. All I saw was a beautiful, golden tail waving at me from on top of the hill. Now what? The hill was so steep, how can I get up there? How did *he* get up there? I said, "Here, come, d-—!" He even turned around, looking right at me, and I swear I heard, *"I can't help myself! It's a dog thing."* I managed to climb halfway up when he came down with me. Back on the leash he went; back to square one, again.

I had heard that agility training was good for discipline, as well as off-leash commands, so we signed up. I'm not sure he liked all the obstacles, but he was a trooper, following my leads as he went through the course. He was not the fastest car on the track; the Aussies ran circles around him, which was all right. We weren't here to win medals; we were just here to have fun. It was his turn to go through the tunnel. He went in, while I ran to the other end to be ready to give him his next direction, but he didn't come out as quickly as he went in.

Where was he? The trainer looked and waited. I looked and waited. The tunnel moved as if he was stuck, but that couldn't be. Here came Brady prancing out of the tunnel toward us, proud as could be, with a stick in his mouth! He is a golden retriever, after all. He retrieved all right, but where he found the stick in that tunnel is *still* a mystery. A thought came through to me again: *What's the problem? No one else found a stick but me. Aren't you proud, Mom?* I heard this and just laughed. But *did* a thought of his come through to me? It must be my imagination, right? We finished the classes, but clearly, a career in agility was definitely out of the question. I knew there was something special about this dog. Can dogs have a sense of humor?

The Nose Made Me Do It

I can't tell you how many times this thought came through from Brady. Even before I knew of this special connection we have, I would always say to him, "I know, the nose made you do it, right?" Now that I think about it, it was Brady sending me those thoughts already.

I read that the golden retriever had its origin in England, where they were bred to hunt birds for the royals. They bred lots of hunting breeds plus bloodhounds to find a great hunting companion. The golden retriever that developed had a natural instinct to hunt plus a kind and gentle demeanor which made them wonderful family dogs as well.

Brady's nose always got him in trouble. While on a walk, if a door was open to a house, a gate, or a garage, he saw it as an invitation to visit someone. If our front door was open, he felt it was time for a walk, with or without me. He always went to the left. I still cannot figure that out—another mystery of the dog world, I guess—but I knew where to find him. He was never out for long, since I knew he was an escape artist if given the chance. He was just so fast! I found him exploring down the street, having a great time.

Let's try this again. "Here, come," and then I used my loud, deep voice, *"now!"* I said. Surprise, he came; reluctantly, but he came. Again I heard him: *I was still exploring. What's the problem?*

I said to myself, *What is going on? Am I going crazy, or can I really hear this dog? I know he can read my mind, because he is always right by my side when I want to go out, asking me if he can come. Is he sending me his thoughts as well? This has to be my imagination, right?*

The nose continued to get him in trouble. Some examples included finding cat food left by Samantha, a few more episodes in the park, munching on Thanksgiving leftovers, and ending up in the doggie ER. I met some of the nicest people courtesy of Brady running into their house or garage. The best smell I think he liked came from the beach one morning. We'd go to Hendry's Beach, where there was an off-leash area so he could run free, explore, and play with other dogs. We were enjoying a quiet day—sunny, very peaceful, just listening to the waves and the birds. We were there early, so there were not too many people or dogs. All alone, strolling on the sand with my faithful companion by my side, I was thinking, *Isn't this wonderful,* when up went his nose. I could see it twitching, and I knew: he had picked up a scent. I smelled it too, only I did not like the smell.

Brady ran down the beach in a flash, and of course, I ran after him, knowing he would get there way before I did and get into some kind of trouble. There it was, and Brady was rubbing himself all over a dead seal. Now *that* was a smell! I put his leash on him, and back to the car we went. No way could we continue our walk with a smell so potent it made my eyes tear. We only lived twenty minutes from the beach, but this morning, it was the longest ride home. All the windows of the car were down, but still my eyes burned. We were stopped at a traffic light, and I swear that the car next to us could smell him too. They rolled up their window, while Brady just had what looked like a big grin on his face.

I heard him again: *What a great find, Mom!* His thought, definitely not mine. Three shampoos and doggie deodorant later, there was no whiff of the seal. Then I heard it, the first time I knew it was really Brady's thought: *Stop fussing. I'm a dog, and that was a great smell. Now I smell like flowers, yuck!* I actually turned toward him, asking, "Brady, was that you?" He just titled his head, as if to add, *It's about time you really heard me.*

Mud, Mischief, and the Mad Dash

After Brady had been staying with his friend Rusty, we'd come home, and it was always a mad dash to our back yard. We were both running, but of course, it was Brady who found the "gift" from Samantha in the dirt first. "Brady! This really is disgusting," I said.

I don't get it; must be another mystery of the dog world. We'd be upstairs on my bed, taking a nap, when up went his nose. I knew what that meant. He was scenting another gift from Samantha. He ran down the stairs, into the back yard, always beating me to the gift. I don't know how he could smell it from so far away, but he did. It took years until he finally lost interest in—you know what. Luckily I had a doggie toothbrush and toothpaste on hand at all times. And luckily he never learned to lick anyone.

We walked twice a day, whether it was sunny or rainy, it didn't matter. We met many people on our walks. Most had dogs, but some did not; they just wanted to meet Brady. Actually, they didn't have a choice. He would pull me over and stop them on the sidewalk until they acknowledged him. I still see and am friends with all the people he's picked up on his travels. One of his greatest pleasures was checking out the "neighborhood newspaper" on all the trees and bushes along our route. I always wondered what information they offered, maybe neighborhood gossip, but it was, for sure, another dog thing.

A few times, he didn't want to go on the way we were heading. I didn't know why, but I always trusted his instincts, so we would turn around to take a different path. He stayed by my side as he got older, even sharing my umbrella if we got caught in a downpour. When he was a puppy, he would find the largest mud puddle at the school and walk right into it. Therefore the garden hose became my best friend. I think his paws had magnets that attracted dirt and burrs.

It had been raining for days, and the ground was soaked in mud. Brady walked out back, deciding to bury his latest bone, only I didn't see him until he came back into the dining room. "Brady!" I screamed. There were muddy paw prints all over. The more I tried to corral him to take him back outside, the more he thought it was a game, shaking off the excess mud. How far can mud splatter? Let me count the ways—the hallway carpet, the hallway walls, the table, the chairs, the dining room walls, the hutch, the kitchen floor, the cabinets; shall I go on? Mud, mud everywhere. I literally didn't know what to do. He was having such a good time, I just started to laugh and couldn't stop; a stress reliever, I guess. Where do I start? Do I let the mud dry, or do I try to wash things off now? *First things first,* I thought. *Get him outside and get my trusted garden hose. The mud will still be there when we come back in.* On all fours, I started to clean up the mud, with him thinking I was playing with him, getting in my face with a toy.

Hours later, Gary came home and said, "How was your day? Did you have a nice, cozy afternoon?"

"Don't ask." I said.

Brady always told us when he had to go out. Even in the middle of the night, he came to my side of the bed; he didn't bark, he just made a guttural sound like HUMMMMMM? OUUUUT? Very polite, he was. This night was very peaceful, quiet, and warm, with a sky full of stars. I started to look for a shooting star as I waited for him to finish. In the next moment, the silence was broken by a whine and a whimpering, and then I smelled it. "Oh, no!" I shrieked. "Gary, Gary!" In the corner of the yard, I saw a little animal with black eyes, fuzzy black fur, and a beautiful, perfect white stripe down its back and tail. It is a cute creature, except when it is in your yard, and having a smell one never forgets, especially if it is on your beloved pet. Gary came tearing down the stairs, knowing exactly what had happened with one whiff of the night air. Brady was skunked! *Now what?* I thought. It was 2:00 in the morning. We couldn't leave him outside all night; he was not used to that—but we couldn't bring him inside either.

I'd heard you can bathe them in tomato juice, but where would we find any at this hour? Gary got dressed, saying he'd get some somewhere. I rinsed off Brady's face, got the shampoo, and proceeded to give him a bath, with which he was *not* pleased. Twenty minutes later, Gary returned with a carton of four large containers of tomato juice. "Where in the world did you get those?" I asked.

"Denny's is open twenty-four hours, so I asked for tomato juice," he replied. I wonder what the waiter thought of this request. We proceeded to wash our dog in our front yard in tomato juice. We couldn't wash him in the back yard because he would lick the juice off the ground in the morning, and that would definitely not be a good thing. I'm not sure who had more juice on them, Brady or us, but after he decided to shake, I knew it was us. I rinsed him off while it was Gary's job to keep him from licking the juice off his fur. We brought him inside to dry as we tried to get back to sleep, but even with all the windows wide open, there was not enough air freshener to clear the air. Next morning, the front lawn looked like something out of a horror flick, so out came my trusted garden hose again. Our lawn was the most beautiful green in about two weeks. Think about this, Miracle Green—maybe there's a new fertilizer in the making?

The next morning, I went to the pet store for another lotion, which did help, but it took a good three weeks before we had company over. Luckily, this was our only encounter with this creature of the night.

Brady and his siblings. Who's who?

Home where he belongs

"I'm the boss!" said Samantha

Blossom being a meerkat

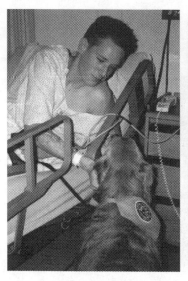

Brady with a patient   A proud therapy dog

Visiting a classroom

Rusty and Brady exercising

Rusty, Brady and Daisy

Mud, mud everywhere!

Big Sam

Brady, Maddy, and Cody

It's a three-dog night

Zack,   Luke

Miss Zoe

Samantha and Brady—"friends"

BRADY'S FAMILY

Gary, Brady, and Doris

Brady's little blue car

Christmas 2010

Friends

Brady had many friends in the neighborhood. Eric and Samantha, two children who lived down the street, would come to play with him, as they learned what it takes to own a dog. My children were grown, so Brady was always so happy to see them. Six months later, their family adopted their own golden, named Casey, and we quickly became good friends through our dogs. We often walked together while our dogs seemed to share a secret language that only they could understand. I wonder if they talked about the morning newspaper they had encountered, sharing news about the neighborhood, just as we did.

When Casey was excited to see you, his whole body would wiggle. He was one of the sweetest and happiest dogs I knew; I called him my god-dog.

Sam, a big, black Bouvier des Flandres, looked like a bear walking down the street. He was another of Brady's best friends. Sam didn't really like other dogs, and he *really* didn't like cats or skateboards, but for some reason, he liked Brady. His owner Evie, Gary, and I became fast friends, especially since we were all from New York.

It's a New York connection. We walked many afternoons together, our two dogs walking in sync, as if they were old souls that had known each other for a long time.

Brady loved to explore and was always looking for new routes, so we would take Evie and Sam on our adventures. Of course, Sam was always on the lookout for a cat or a skateboard, and Evie was looking for a lamppost to hang on to, should Sam find either one. We would go to her house or to our house, and Big Sam would actually do a little tap dance when he saw Brady, as if to say, *here comes my very own friend.* When Sam passed away, Brady would not want to walk in front of his house for the longest time. I think he knew Sam was gone, and he missed him and their special friendship.

While I was preparing for this book, Evie and I talked about our special boys. She shared some pictures of Sam as a puppy when he was at the blessing of Bouviers by one of the Brothers of Mt. Calvary in Montecito. There was a picture from October 1994 of Sam and our friend, Brother Allen, bestowing the blessing. Gary and I used to go up to Mt. Calvary with Brady to visit. Allen loved Brady and let him have the run of the monastery, inside and out. We'd sit in the courtyard, high on the mountaintop overlooking beautiful Santa Barbara and the ocean, as Brady attempted to catch lizards or anything else that moved. I brought out a picture of Allen with Brady at our house from May 2004, and we both agreed it must have been fate that we met. It really is a small world after all.

One of Brady's first friends was a beautiful golden named Rusty, whom we met at the grammar school located behind our homes.

She would become a regular guest at our house when her owners went away, and Brady was able to go to her house when we went away. Through our dogs, we again had new friends, Kathy and Mike. Rusty had a pool where she and Brady would go swimming during the summer. Rusty, being a real lady, would gently step into the water to retrieve a ball. Brady would step cautiously into the pool after the ball, but Rusty out swam him every time. She just glided through the water with ease and grace. Lazy afternoons would be spent in our back yard, with Rusty lying on one lounge chair, Brady on the other; they then went to the pool for a cooling swim.

A few years later, Rusty had a litter of golden puppies. They kept one, naming her Daisy, and I think Brady had a little crush on her. She could outrun and out swim them all, and she had the best cannonball off the side of the pool you ever saw! When we would bring the girls home, Daisy was the first though the door, out into the pool, with a great big cannonball splash. This was sheer heaven to her.

Our daughter and her husband had a German shorthair dog, Miss Cody. She was a beautiful, sleek girl with long eyelashes. She always wanted to snuggle, and she had a personality that you couldn't help but love. Along came Miss Madelyn, also a German shorthair. When she and Brady played, Maddy would run circles around Brady, always getting to the ball first. Finally Brady would just lie down, letting Maddy get the ball, as if to say, *Why bother?*

When Cody and Maddy would come to our house, Maddy could curl up into the smallest ball, pretending to be sound sleep; after all, securing the perimeter of the house for hours is exhausting. Then,

35

after a while, when she relaxed, one leg would pop out, then the next, and then the last two, until she was all stretched out, finally relaxed. She was like a jack-in-the-box, popping out all over. They were two of the most beautiful bookends, and sweet to match.

They also had a cat named PJ, who never liked me. When my daughter and I picked him out at the animal shelter, we were told he had been declawed, but when we brought him home and I picked him up, he dug his claws into the carpet so deeply, I literally had to pluck each toe, with the nail, out of the carpet. I think he never forgave me for that, almost as if I found out his secret that he really *did* have claws.

Now there is Zack, a handsome black Lab with fur so sleek and shiny, he looks as if he gets a daily coat of shellac. Also in their household is a shy rescue named Luke. I nicknamed him Lucky Dog, because he has a new life with so much love and attention. He's come a long way. He has the most beautiful markings, one being a brown spot the shape of a heart on his back. Along with a cat named Balou and a now a beautiful new baby girl, our granddaughter completes their family.

Our son and his wife have a little cutie named Zoe, a Chihuahua that is also a rescue who survived parvo and kennel cough. She is beautiful and light-brown with a bare belly because of the parvo. She is all of six pounds, with springs under her feet. She can jump three feet straight up onto anything and runs very quickly—here one minute, gone the next. Zoe runs circles around Brady as well, and yes, she gets to the toys first. (Do I see a pattern here? Brady is either lazy or very smart to let all the other dogs do all the running to get toys.) Having such a tiny dog around, as opposed to Brady, I am always afraid I'll lock her in a closet or the fridge or step on her. She has quite the wardrobe, including pink Doggles (a brand name of goggles for dogs) for their speedboat. She is a love.

Brady had many other furry four-footed friends in the neighborhood: Winston, Remington, Harley, Daisy, Shamus, Truman, Sadie, just to name a few, and yes, a dog named Bingo! Bingo was a dog that we always saw at Goleta Beach, where the three of us would have a relaxing picnic lunch on the weekends. We would be listening to the waves, feeling the warm breeze, and the next thing we knew, we were all taking a nap. Daphne and her brother, Toby—who was called Wilber—still live on our street. Then there is a standard black poodle named Butler. His name suits him perfectly, for he is stately, handsome, very smart, and funny. He is also a thief, having eaten an entire wheel of brie at his owner's dinner party. He has also helped himself to stockings and various other elastic items.

And then there is Burt. He is a beautiful tabby cat that had an obsession with Brady. I babysat him and his siblings one day, putting them all in our family room. When Brady came in with me, Burt started to bite his legs and his tail, jumping on him as if he wanted to play. I guess Burt thought Brady was just a large cat, since he had never met a dog before. Brady tried to get away, but Burt just kept playing with his tail and his hind legs. It was a funny sight. I heard Brady's thought: *Let me out of here. This cat is crazy!*

Over the years, Samantha mellowed, becoming friends with Brady too. Sometimes they even slept side by side on our bed or the couch. On a warm summer day, they shared a lounge chair and seemed perfectly content. Brady still tried to get Samantha's food, but now she just let him. He was a great help around the house in picking up leftover cat food—or any food for that matter. His name should have been Hoover.

Just Passing Through

People who know me know of my love for animals. I was always taking care of dogs or cats, finding lost dogs and trying to get them home. We've had many strange dogs in our back yard waiting for their owners to pick them up. We would just find them running around without their owners, so Brady would invite them home with us. We found the same two dogs twice and had to call their owners to come get them.

While looking out our front window one afternoon, I noticed there were two dogs barking under our tree. Going outside to check on the commotion, I saw that they had our Samantha trapped in that tree. The dogs were relentless, as they were determined to get her. I had a bright idea; at least I thought it was bright at the time. I'll just look at their collars and call the owner to get them, as I've done with strange dogs before. There was only one problem: the cute cocker spaniel wasn't wearing a collar; only the other dog did, *a Great Dane! You look like a nice dog,* I thought. I heard Great Danes are really gentle giants, right? *Okay, big boy, let's see where you belong.*

I managed to get the phone number with all ten fingers intact, and I called, but of course, no one was home. *Now what?* I thought. They were still salivating over my cat when I had another bright idea: let's see if I can get them in my car so I can drive them home. Meanwhile, Brady was watching from the front window, looking at me as I heard his thought: *Are you crazy?* I opened the door to my car. "Let's go, guys." Lo and behold, they jumped in, so off we went. Of course the Great Dane, being great and all, jumped in the front seat. I didn't know how he fit in that seat, but he did. Driving around our neighborhood, I found the owners in front of their house looking for their dogs. When they saw me coming around the corner, they just laughed. I guess it was a pretty funny picture, or were they laughing at how stupid I was to have strange dogs in my car, especially when one was a Great Dane.

One afternoon when Brady and I were walking with Evie past their house, we heard a very low, deep bark. Evie said, "That sounds like a big dog."

I said, "It is; it's a Great Dane, and I know because he was in my car."

When I told her the story, she politely replied, "That may not have been one of your best ideas." I think someone else told me that.

Brady tilted his head and I heard, *"I told you so."*

I took care of some cats for my neighbors next door when they were away, and I fell in love with them too: two rag dolls, Lucy and Vinnie, a beauty named Coco, and a tabby named Motor. They were all indoor cats, except Motor thought otherwise, wanting to go out every morning.

On a dark, rainy day, Gary left early for work, as Samantha was still asleep in her bed, with Brady sleeping on the other side in his bed. I was curled up, waiting for the alarm clock to signal 7 a.m. My alarm clock was Brady, because somehow he always knew when it was 7 a.m. and 4 p.m., which meant time for a walk. Samantha had a strange purr that morning while walking over me, but when I looked in her bed, she was still asleep. *What is in bed with me?* I sat up, as Motor was making himself at home. I guess his owners couldn't find him before work to bring him back inside. Since it was raining, he had found the cat door in our garage and came on in. Smart cat! Brady and Samantha didn't move, as if it was normal that Motor was in this house.

That's what started a special relationship with Motor the cat. He came and went as he pleased. Sometimes he stayed a short time; sometimes he stayed all day. I can't tell you how many times Don or Shari, his owners, would call or come over, asking, "Is Motor with you?" And sure enough, he was asleep someplace nice and warm, taking his sweet time to be found. Outside, Samantha and Motor slept on one lounge chair, with Brady on the other. I would squeeze in with Brady; Gary with the cats. I wish I had a picture of that. When friends or family were here, Motor would come strolling through the house as if he owned it. I guess he did in a way. I loved it, and simply explained, "That's just Motor passing through." He was one in a million. Burt, the silly cat that loved Brady, was part of this family after they lost their sweet Motor.

Two little pugs live in our neighborhood, Willie and Otis. Of course, Brady became friends with them too, always stopping to visit when we saw them. We were coming home late from running errands one afternoon when we saw Willie and Otis running free, into the street, all over the place, but where was Bob? I stopped the car, as it was starting to get dark with raindrops beginning to fall. I couldn't just leave them running free. Another bright idea! I called, "Willie, Otis. Here, boys." They came right to me, and into my car they went. In the back seat was Brady, riding shotgun, while Willie and Otis were running under his legs, jumping over his back, up to me in the front seat, and back again.

I figured Bob must be around here somewhere, looking for them. I didn't know where they live, so I just drove around to see if I could spot him. Half an hour went by with no sign of Bob. I asked everyone we saw if they have seen anyone looking for pugs, but no one had. I started to take them home with me when around the corner came a station wagon with two women yelling out the front windows. They saw Willie looking out my window and screeched to a stop. I stopped as well as they came running to my car. "You found our babies!" they cried. These two pugs were *not* Willie and Otis; they were two strange dogs in my car with my Brady! Three dogs that had never met before in one car, and Brady was a trooper again, going along with another one of my bright ideas. With lots of hugs and kisses from the owners, there was a happy ending. They were visiting friends around the corner when the dogs escaped. Then I heard thoughts of wisdom from my dog: *Maybe you should stop having your great ideas, huh?*

"Wise guy." I said to him.

No Strangers Here

I always knew that Brady had a special gift. No matter where we went, people just wanted to meet him. My daughter heard of dogs going to the hospital to cheer people up. I thought this was a great idea, since he loved meeting people. I checked with our local hospital to find out when the next test was to be given and what would be involved. This was what we were meant to do; I just knew it. Was this Brady's thought again or mine? Well, of course, it had to be mine, right? Years later, I would learn how wrong I was. This was Brady's plan all along.

Being on our best behavior, we took the test. Things went pretty well, so I thought, *okay, we're going to nail this!* Even though Brady was only a year and a half old, the woman who gave the test said we were a good team and she would pass us. I was excited, and I guess Brady sensed this—jumping up toward the woman who gave the test. His collar scratched her arm. *Oh no,* I thought, *we blew it.* Even Brady hung his head as if in shame. She looked at him and then at me as she dabbed her arm. A smile came across her face as she passed us anyway. She said, "This is a special dog. I can see it in his eyes. He'll make a difference." Oh how right she was.

Gary and I were teaching confirmation at the time and went to a place called Hillside House as a group activity for the kids. Of course, we brought our Brady. He had a lot of puppy in him and still needed a lot of discipline. We were walking down the hall of the facility with him; he was looking for any food someone might have dropped, not really paying attention to much of anything else—or me, for that matter. When people came out of their rooms to meet him, the response to Brady was overwhelming. Everyone wanted to pet him or hug him, and of course, the nurses gave him kisses and, yes, lipstick ended up on his forehead. One nurse came over to tell me that there was a special patient who hadn't spoken in three months, and perhaps Brady could be of comfort to him. The nurse put David's hand on Brady's fur as we all stood very still, watching. David leaned over his wheelchair to put his arm around the dog and said, "I love you, Brady," a moment I will never forget. I cried, as did the staff, while David tried to smile. That's when I knew this was our calling.

We joined a national pet therapy organization called Love on a Leash. *How beautifully fitting,* I thought. After his special vest and ID arrived from them, we were off for our photo ID badges for Santa Barbara Cottage Hospital.

Our first official visit as a pet therapy team was to Goleta Valley Cottage Hospital, where we made our first mistake. Brady found out which nurses' station had treats, and from then on, his first mission coming through the doors was to drag me to that nurses' station for his cookie. Only then could he concentrate on meeting people. I know he loved coming here, because he always seemed to have a smile on his face. What's not to like about this job? He was the center of attention, everyone petted him, and patients wanted to feed him their lunch. To that I said *thanks, but no thanks,* because he had allergies to certain foods.

We started at Goleta Valley Cottage, which was close to home, as well as smaller than the main hospital. We came two days a week, Tuesdays and Thursdays, one hour at a time. For every hour Brady would work, he'd sleep for two. The concentration and attention he learned to give to the staff and the patients was amazing. When we entered a room, he first went to the patient, putting his head where they could pet him, sometimes staying quite a while. Patient and dog stared right into each other's eyes, as if there was a secret being shared. Other times he left the patient rather quickly and went to one of the visitors, leaning into them as if to say, *Things will be all right.* I later realized that many times it was a son or daughter, as the patient and the parents just needed Brady's reassurance and unconditional love.

He was constantly amazing me with his instincts of meeting the needs of humans. We were able to get to know many of the staff members, since we went on a regular basis. One afternoon, it was very quiet and slow at the hospital when down the hall I heard, "Will Brady Clancy please report to the nurses' station." It was one of the few times we forgot to get his cookie. That'll teach us.

Halfway through our rounds was the physical therapy office, where we met many nice people as well. One, a therapist named Wendy, always knew if Brady was thirsty. She even gave him his very own water bowl with his name on it. Actually, it was a basin for use in case someone felt nauseated, if you know what I mean. Brady just thought this was *his* bowl and was happy to have water. Everyone we met made us feel loved and at home; they were always very happy to see us.

As the years went by, all I had to say to Brady was, "It's time to go to work," and he would go over to his vest. We found ourselves staying at this small hospital. They considered Brady their dog, and we considered this *our* hospital. He was always excited to get into a room to visit, except for one time in the nine and a half years we volunteered there. The patient was ill but still wanted very much to pet him, but Brady didn't want to go into that room. I couldn't figure it out. I apologized as I said, "He must be tired, as it's almost time to go home." I told Gary that night how odd that was of Brady. Next week, one of the nurses informed me the same patient suddenly passed away that evening. Did he sense death? I've heard of other animals doing this. He amazed me again.

One afternoon, after coming out of ICU, a large family was in the waiting room. Of course, when Brady saw them, he had to go in for a visit. We performed our usual tricks: spin, down, up, sit, the weave, walking between my feet as I walked, cookie on the nose and don't take, cookie on the floor and don't take. I carried a bell on a rope with me, holding it to the side, and said, "Dinner." Then he came over and hit it with his nose till it rang. This was fun to practice, especially when we had company over at our house for dinner, as Brady the butler rang the dinner bell. We would end each performance with a nice, wet, slobbery kiss on my cheek.

Of course, after much applause, it was time to meet and greet the audience. He proceeded to go around the room, standing in front of each person until they acknowledged him. Then he came to his greatest challenge: the man who didn't like dogs. He didn't even want to look at Brady, let alone touch him. Brady was relentless with determination to win him over. He stared at the man, inching a little closer, one small step at a time until he was in the man's face. The man kept saying, "No, no," but Brady would not give up. Finally the man took one finger and touched Brady's forehead. Well, that's all it took for Brady to full-on nuzzle up to the man who didn't like dogs. Now came two fingers and then the full pat with both hands. Brady had won again! "He's okay," the man said as everyone laughed. One of the women said he was forty-five years old and had never touched a dog before. We had many adventures and have wonderful memories in this little hospital of ours.

Brady loved children, but there wasn't a children's ward at this hospital. A friend volunteered at Mountain View Elementary School in special education and mentioned that her children might like to see Brady, since some of them have never met a dog before. She took some pictures of Brady from hospital visits to the teacher's lounge with a sign-up sheet for classroom visits. The response was wonderful, as many classes wanted to meet him. We also ended up going to many different elementary schools, talking to children about pet therapy, caring for pets, and, of course, performing our tricks. As we talked about caring for animals, the children shared stories about their pets—what kind they had, what their names were, and what tricks they could do.

The younger children always wanted to see Brady's teeth, some pushing up his lips with their fingers for a closer look. He couldn't figure out why his teeth were of such interest. He tilted his head as his thought came through: *What's with my teeth? I don't want to see their teeth.* This was the perfect introduction for our next segment, the importance of brushing one's teeth. It's so important, even a dog does it. I would whip out his toothbrush, making sure I told them that this toothpaste was especially made for dogs adding, DO NOT TRY THIS AT HOME. I could just see the children getting their toothbrush at home tonight, trying to brush their pet's teeth. Brady was so patient letting me do this to him, I think he knew how the kids loved this when he heard their laughter. Pictures were always taken with all the children around this dog. He was a real ham for the camera and seemed to know just when to smile. Then in the mail came priceless thank you letters from the children. His birth family always called him the "over achiever" in the litter of puppies; how true that was to be. We also visited special education classes through United Cerebral Palsy. Most of the children didn't have dogs, and some had never petted one, so it was always a treat for them to meet Brady.

Brady had lots of health issues. He had chronic foot boils due to allergies, several surgeries and had to have a special diet. All the dogs in the neighborhood knew the sound of the UPS truck, and Carlos, the driver, did not disappoint them. He always had a treat for the dogs in his truck, but because of Brady's allergies, we had to devise a plan. Carlos would drive by and I would throw a cookie from my pocket onto the sidewalk as if Carlos had done it and Brady was happy. I never did ask Brady if he knew about the switch.

Two years ago he had two lumps removed and the small one was diagnosed as apocrine sweat gland carcinoma. Cancer. We were devastated as we took him to a veterinary oncologist. The treatment recommended was eighteen days of radiation with no guarantee to kill all the cancer. We said no, Brady would not understand why he would have to be in pain and discomfort. We took him home and would have him tested every six months with extensive blood work as well as checking for any unusual lumps. We didn't know what the future holds for any of us, but to put him through that was unthinkable. He wouldn't be able to go to the hospital, the beach, the bank, lunches with us—all the things he loved. His world would stop for several months, and I know he would not want that. We decided to love him and take him with us even more, to enjoy whatever time we had. We prayed we would be together for many, many more years, hopeful that the cancer would never come back.

Working the Room

People were drawn to this dog, always by my side. His eyes would look directly into your soul, as he seemed to understand what you needed. We learned to communicate through thought, so I knew we had a special connection. I just didn't know how special our journey would ultimately become. No matter where we went or who we met, they all said the same thing: it was his eyes. He was a comfort immediately and soothed many a person who didn't even like dogs, was afraid, or was just having a bad day. Even the grumpiest person mellowed by just petting him, and they always ended up with a smile. He could work a room like a politician.

Going to the bank always took the longest time, because he would pull me over to the waiting line before I could even start my transaction. I couldn't believe the thought that came through one day: *These people are too uptight. Let's smell them and see how we can help.* I bent down, whispering to Brady, "I heard what you said. We can help, sure, but you do the smelling. If I do, we will end up in jail." He cocked his head as if to ask, *why.* I just said, "It's a human thing; trust me."

Sure enough, he visited them all, one by one. To some he would just say hello; with others he would linger and lean against them as if to say,

"I'm here for you." Every person smiled in his presence and was not in a hurry or impatient anymore. Some would come to us just to ask to hug him, and some would cry into his fur, saying, "This is just what I needed, because I lost my dog last month." Somehow he always received a hug, a pat, lipstick on his forehead, and an invitation to come home with them. This became a weekly ritual. All the tellers got to know him, and when we came in, it was always, "Hello, Brady!"

Every week he greeted all who were in line or were coming in. One young man from the bank said, "He is a better greeter than I am; we should give him a job." At the end of each visit, the same thought came through: *Thanks for taking me, Mom. A good day. Where can we go next?*

Restaurants were always fun. He was a welcome guest on their outdoor patio and had the staff eating out of his paw! Other guests wanted to say hello too, since he was very polite and didn't bother with any other dogs that were there dining. He enjoyed his doggie ice cream for his lunch and then settling in for a quick snooze under the table. There was one occasion when the temptation was just too great. My pancakes were served a little too close to his nose, and in the next moment, the pancakes were gone. Brady had the funniest expression on his face, smacking his lips while trying to swallow the unexpected treat, as another thought came to me: *Some syrup would have helped!*

"Sorry, Brady, all you can have is water," I said.

Then I heard: *I'll take anything! And tell the cook they were dry!* I'm beginning to think this dog has a sense of humor.

Driving Mr. Brady

I would be getting dressed upstairs as he was sleeping in the foyer downstairs. Not even talking out loud, I would think to myself, *I have to go to the store,* or wherever, and before I knew it, he was behind me, saying, *Can I come? Please, can I come?* Gary thinks I must have a routine, like the hairdryer or something to alert him, but I don't know. I tried different routines, and he always knew when I was ready to go out. And if I was just going to stay home, he would stay asleep in the foyer. Makes me wonder.

I have an SUV in which Brady liked to ride shotgun, his hind legs on the back seat, with his front paws on the front center console. I can't tell you how many kisses were blown to him from girls in passing cars. When we were stopped at a traffic light, they would roll down their window, here comes the kiss, and then, "Hi there, handsome!" I told him, "You are a babe magnet." I swear he had a smile on those big lips. We were on our way to one of our favorite places, the beach, one afternoon, when I found out that this dog *did* have a sense of humor. We were stopped at a traffic light on the overpass, and coming toward us was a woman with, let's say, a very large chest that was bouncing quite a lot. Brady looked directly at her, as did I, and he then turned to me, and his thought was: *Did you see those _____?*

"Brady O'Shea Clancy," I said, "you are a dog!" This was the funniest thought that had come through to me.

When he was riding shotgun, at times people would park next to us, saying that it looked as if the dog was driving the car. When he got older, he liked to sit on the back seat, directly behind me. Many times on our trips, someone in the parking lot would come over to us, saying that he looked so regal and stately sitting behind me, as if I was his chauffeur. I would always laugh and say, "Yes, I'm driving Mr. Brady." I could see him in the back seat with a smirk on his face. He especially enjoyed riding in my little blue convertible, with the wind in his ears and his big golden tail over the back seat as if he was waving at everyone. There was only a small bench in the back of my car, just barely enough space for him to stand or sit. One day, a big, buff man in a huge pickup truck pulled up next to us at a traffic light and said, "You're gonna need a bigger car!" and then laughed out loud as he pulled away. We attracted a lot of attention, lots of funny comments, always smiles and, of course, more kisses blown out the windows of passing cars for Brady than you can imagine.

Fire!

July 1, 2008 was a hot, dry day as the fire started in the mountains. It became known as the Gap Fire, burning 9,443 acres and four outbuildings. Thankfully, neither homes nor lives were lost. Gary and I were becoming concerned because we could see the fire growing from our upstairs window. Since my friend Evie was in Europe on vacation, we were worried about her cat, Blossom, at home. A friend was taking care of her but lived quite a distance from Evie's house. If an evacuation order came through, she would not be able to get to Blossom. The fire was growing, and I was becoming increasingly nervous about the possibly of having to evacuate, so I started to pack up the car that afternoon.

I loaded a few paintings, checkbooks, business papers, medications, cat food, cat litter box, dog food, carrier for Samantha, and I went down to Evie's house to get Blossom. I put her in one of the bedrooms with her carrier, so if we had to leave, she would be ready to come with us. Taking a walk late that afternoon, Gary and I could see the fire approaching the ridge and thought to ourselves that this does not look good. When we came home, we put more things in the car and had clothes by the front door. Sure enough, the evacuation order came, and we had to get out quickly. I grabbed Samantha and

Brady, and Gary got Blossom and our clothes as we piled into the car. We headed for Santa Ynez, to our daughter's mother-in-law's house, where our family members who live in Goleta planned to meet if an evacuation order came. We all arrived, exhausted but safe.

Shirley graciously welcomed us into to her home with a much-appreciated glass of wine. In the house were eight adults, two children, six dogs, and four cats! It was like Noah's Ark, seeking refuge in a flood, only this was a firestorm. Everyone got along, humans and animals alike. Our bedroom housed Gary and me, our three critters, two litter boxes, three food trays, and three water bowls. Samantha slept under the bed, Blossom slept under the covers, and Brady slept in between the litter boxes, hoping for a late-night snack. Brady's thought; *A bit crowded in here, don't you think?*

And me? I didn't sleep much, because I was listening for that scratching sound and preparing to get to the litter box first. Here were two strange cats that had never met before, in one bedroom for almost three days, and they both survived with all their fur, ears, whiskers, and tails. Brady still had his nose and eyes intact without scratches or the need for plastic surgery. He was able to get outside during the day and play with the other dogs, but all the cats in the house were confined to their respective rooms. We were able to go home the morning of the third day and found our neighborhood in good shape. We had lots of ashes, but that was okay, considering what some people come home to after a fire. The fire was finally contained at the end of July.

"Mommy I Don't Feel Good"

And so the final chapter begins . . .

I received the thought while I was upstairs getting ready for bed. I knew it was from Brady; he was sick. When I came downstairs, I saw that he was in the foyer, not wanting to get up. He hadn't eaten much of his dinner that night, which was odd, because he always had a typical dog appetite. His eyes were different, and I could tell he wasn't feeling well.

I tried to coax him upstairs, but he wouldn't come, even for his special cookie. I knew something was wrong and told Gary I'd have to take him to La Cumbra Animal Hospital the next morning. I slept on the floor with him all night, feeling very glad when morning came, so I could call the doctor. They said to bring him right in. This was Monday morning, March 21, 2011. The doctor at that time said she thought it was pancreatitis and that he had to stay in the hospital for an IV drip of fluids, with tests to confirm. During the exam, she felt that his liver was enlarged as well. She recommended an ultrasound, telling us the technician who performs this test will be here this Wednesday.

In the meantime, I was in touch with our regular veterinarian, who said he would be there to supervise the test and call me with the results. I was able to take Brady home that night, but he didn't want to eat. I made him chicken and rice, but he only ate a handful. I slept by his side again. Tuesday morning, we were back at the hospital for more fluids. The house was so empty without him; I couldn't wait to pick him up that afternoon. Wednesday morning, I brought him back for more fluids and the ultrasound, feeling that something was really wrong with our boy. I came home very restless, pacing, with this uneasy feeling all day. Then the phone call came.

March 23: two large tumors on his liver, some bleeding in his spleen, his kidneys were not functioning completely, along with confirmed pancreatitis. I was devastated. Not our boy; it's too soon! The tears came, and I couldn't stop. I could barely tell Gary over the phone. I knew the tumors might be cancer, since he was a cancer survivor two years ago to the month. Picking him up that night, I still couldn't believe he was so sick. We had the option to go to a large animal hospital in Ventura for exploratory surgery to confirm the cancer. But if it was cancer, they wouldn't do anything because of where the tumors were located. Plus then he would have to suffer with a large incision in the time he had left.

His prognosis was not good. His organs were slowly shutting down, and it was just a matter of time. It could be months or a week. How much time we had with him, we just didn't know. We were in shock. *He'll only be eleven in May; that's still young, isn't it?* We didn't want to accept this. We talked some more with the doctor and decided to take Brady home, to just love him, be with him, and go to our favorite places for as long as we could. With his organs in trouble too, putting him through surgery might possibly postpone the inevitable a few months, but we needed to think about *him*. We just couldn't stand it if we let his last days be filled with pain and confusion.

With the IV drips he had received at the hospital and a special diet, the pain from the pancreatitis seemed to be under control. He appeared to be comfortable and didn't seem to be in any pain from his other ailments.

That night, he did eat—not with gusto, but he ate—which gave us the false sense of hope that maybe there had been a mistake, that things were not really this bad. That night, reality set in; just looking at him and being with him, we knew. The next morning, I called the doctor and asked how I would know when it was time to let him go. He just said I would know, and he was right, because I knew Brady would tell me. I slept next to him again that night, talking to my boy, while crying in his fur. I kissed his forehead, saying, "You are the best puppy. I love you so much. You helped so many people throughout your life; you comforted them, listened to their secrets, and let them cry in your fur. You always knew who needed your attention the most. You would look directly into their eyes as you understood their pain, then eagerly leaned against them, giving them your unconditional love. Everyone you saw you wanted to meet, and anyone who saw you wanted to meet you. You are and always will be loved by so many."

I told him he was very sick, and it would be time to say good-bye soon. I also promised him that Daddy and I would not let him suffer or be in pain just so he could stay with us a little longer. As I let go of holding him, he looked so deeply and intensely into my eyes, his soul into my soul, that I knew he understood me.

We went for walks on the beach, because he loved the smells. We still went on our two regular walks every day, just much shorter ones, and he came with us to our favorite places for lunch. We called some special friends whom he loved to tell them what was going on. When they came to visit, he was still excited to see every one of them. He loved to ride in my little car with his ears in the wind, so we went for a ride every day. We were blessed that we had a few extra days to love him, to talk to him, just to have him with us. He was sitting with me on the lounge chair on our patio, as we often did, and I asked him to tell me when it will be time. "Give me a sign or your thought, so I know," I said.

That night, he didn't want to eat. He never had his full appetite back, but he had been eating a little. Tonight was different. It was taking a long time for me to get to sleep since his diagnosis, but I finally drifted off from sheer exhaustion.

March 31, 2011, 6 a.m.: I had slept with him on the floor every night since his diagnosis. Daylight was just breaking when I woke up and saw that he was already awake, with his head lying down on his front paws, just looking at me. *It's time.* I asked him if I heard right; was it time? He lifted his head, looked directly into my eyes. Slowly he closed his eyes, held them closed for a moment, and then opened them again, and I knew. It was time to let him go.

Later that morning, we went on our last walk, and I could tell that he was uncomfortable, that pain was setting in. His organs were shutting down. I called the doctor, and he came to the house within the hour. Gary had a very hard time accepting this, because he could not communicate with Brady as I did. I left the two of them alone for a bit, and he too saw that it was time. Somehow Brady told his daddy that his body was sick, he was tired, and he had to go.

The final chapter has been written. Our sweet Brady boy went to sleep March 31, 2011. He died as he lived: at home, with dignity, in my arms and I, in Gary's arms.

The last kiss on his forehead and the last tears in his fur were mine.

The tears came and were uncontrollable. Gary and I have never cried so hard in our lives. Our last gift of love to our boy was to let him go because we knew it was the right thing to do.

With tears streaming down my face, I can barely see the keyboard writing this chapter, as I remember our life together. My sweet little eight-week-old ball of fluff, all the adventures, the mischief, the hospital, all the schools we visited, all the people we met, my partner in our therapy work. The connection we shared is a special gift that not many humans and animals experience together. His gentle spirit was a privilege to share with so many. I miss him still and always will. Gary, too, so loved this special member of our family and still asks, "Where can we go to today where we can bring Brady?" forgetting for a second that he is no longer here.

Having to tell all the people who loved him that he was gone was very painful. There were tears and hugs for weeks when more people found out. It was amazing how many people's lives he touched, as evidenced by the outpouring of love we received by so many heartfelt cards, a book, flowers, plants, and monetary gifts to organizations in his name. He really did make a difference in people's lives, just as the woman who certified him as a therapy pet said he would.

The Monarch Connection

After finishing the previous chapter, I went for a walk around the block by myself. I saw a monarch butterfly again, flying over me twice, leaving as quickly as it had come, as if to say hello. A monarch has visited me many times since Brady died, sometimes sending thoughts, sometimes not.

The afternoon of his death, Gary and I were so devastated, so incredibly sad; we couldn't believe he was gone. We were sitting in silence on a bench in our back yard when I looked up and saw a large, beautiful monarch butterfly flying directly over us as it went to the front of the house. Moments later it came back, this time flying right in front of us. I could feel a whisper of a breeze from its wings brushing against my cheek, as a thought came through: *I'm okay.* It was Brady! I knew it was him sending us a message. I had heard that butterflies can carry spirits of loved ones, especially if there had been a strong connection of love. His spirit and mine, yes, we were connected in a special way. Gary believed it too.

The rest of the afternoon, I was just walking around numb, missing him very much. Seeing his toys, his bowl, his leash, I just had to get out of the house. I went to sit on our patio; knowing we did the right thing didn't make this any easier. I looked up, and here came the monarch again, only this time it stopped, fluttered right in front of my face, and I heard: *Don't be sad, Mommy.* Brady's thought came through again, telling me he is still here.

Two weeks later, Gary and I were coming back from a walk on the beach when a strange rainstorm appeared as we arrived home. No warning, just sudden clouds and then a downpour of rain. Inside the house, I had an incredible urge to take a walk. Gary wasn't sure he wanted to come, but we went. As we were walking down our street, the rain stopped as suddenly as it had started. In front of us appeared the most beautiful full rainbow, very vivid and bright! We looked at each other, both having the same thought. It was Brady going over the rainbow bridge. I had sent friends the rainbow bridge story when they lost a pet, and now Brady was showing us that it is true. His body is young and playful once again, without pain. Walking around the block, Gary and I were in awe at what had just happened. People we met all agreed that this was the strangest rainstorm that came out of nowhere. We just looked at each other, because we knew why it had rained: Brady is still here.

As I was walking down the street with a friend one day, a monarch appeared again, and it seemed to be following us. She even commented how strange it was that he was just staying right with us. But it was not strange to me at all, for I knew it was Brady again. How incredible! He is still here.

Life has been hard without our boy. We both miss him very much, especially when we walk through the front door. The house is so quiet and too clean; no paw prints or fur flying around on the floor, no dog toys to step over. I especially have had a hard time. He was my constant companion, my partner, so it doesn't surprise me that he is contacting me, even after his death. It is just amazing, the connection we still have. Some days are better than others, but then there are moments that trigger a memory, and the tears come.

I hadn't seen a monarch in several weeks. I was walking through the dining room to the kitchen when I saw him! I even did a double take, but he was gone. In a flash, it was my Brady, looking just the way he did when he was young. *Did I imagine this? Did this just happen to me?* I've heard of other people experiencing this, but I never have. As I walked to the back yard in tears, a monarch came again! It flew over to rest on a branch—not a flower—in front of me. I stood very still and whispered, "I saw you, Brady, thank you. I love you." It didn't move off the branch as its wings fluttered very slowly. I just stared at it and then whispered again after a few moments, "I know you have to go," and it flew off just like that. He had sent me another thought; he is still here. This was the most amazing experience I have ever had in my life.

In early October, we went to Kona, Hawaii, to support our son in his Ironman quest. I had often thought of my monarch but had not seen one in quite a while. The house we rented was on a hill that overlooked the ocean, with a beautiful view. I thought Brady would have loved this place. I went out back the first afternoon we were there, admiring all the beautiful flowers, when I saw a monarch butterfly. Do they have monarchs on this island? It flew around me as it had done before, leaving as quickly as it had come. I did not see it again for the rest of our trip. I wonder if he came to look after our son during the Ironman. He loved him very much, so yes, I think that's why he was here. He wanted me to know he would take care of him during the race, and he did. Sean finished with a great time in the World Ironman Championship in Kona.

In my grief, I couldn't remember all the wonderful memories and treasures of our life that I had in my heart. As more months go by, with help, I have been able to look back at our amazing journey. This was not the final chapter of our life together after all, for our work is not done; he has told me that. We will find each other again and be a team. What would my life have been like without this gentle spirit in it? I know I would have had a good life, happy, busy, but would I have had the deep compassion I learned from him, and all these new, wonderful friends? No. The pain in letting him go was the most intense I have ever felt. Would I change the last eleven years? No. I would never have had these incredible experiences and shared a love so deep.

Many people who have loved like this and then had to say good-bye to a beloved companion know exactly how I feel. These wonderful animals are part of us, part of our family. They will always be loved and will forever be in our hearts.

While Gary and I went walking, we would meet someone Gary didn't know but who obviously knew Brady, and I would always say, "Oh, that's another person Brady picked up." Sometimes I even questioned who he wanted us to meet, but I trusted his instinct, and he was never wrong. Strangers became friends that we would see, and still see, in the hospital, UCP, the schools, at the bank, the beach, the stores, and in the neighborhood. Still to this day, I will meet someone I haven't seen in a while, and they will say, "Where's Brady?" I have to tell them, and again the tears come from both of us.

I miss him terribly. There are still moments when I cry in the car or alone at home. I have been able to talk to a lot of people who have helped me through the pain, to understand our special connection and that I'm not crazy to feel these things, to see these monarchs as Brady's spirit. I didn't start out wanting to write a book; I'm just someone who needed to put her feelings into words to be able to move on, to heal my soul. By writing this book, I am trying to celebrate his life and all he gave to so many, not mourn his death. It's hard, but I'm getting there because that's what he wants me to do—to honor his life and remember the life we shared.

Are our spirits soul mates? I don't know. Sometimes I think yes because the connection we had was so deep, it's still here even in death. I was told by someone who believes in the spirit world that Brady would help me write this book, and I believe he did. He has been here with me, still by my side.

This book is a celebration of a gentle soul that touched many lives, especially mine, and left everyone he met with a smile on their face.

Brady's bed is still on one side of our bed, with Samantha's on the other side. Sometimes when I look, I see Samantha sleeping in *his* bed as if to say, "You did win me over."

And I smile.

Oh, what a ride we had!

A Special Sense

Many people walk their dogs past our place. The other day as I worked in the yard, my neighbor Doris walked by with Brady. Brady is a beautiful and gentle Golden Retriever. He always approaches slowly and looks as though he is smiling. He often gives me a little sniff and then nuzzles against me wanting to be petted.

Making small talk I asked if Brady was from the litter of pups born across the street a couple of years ago. She replied affirmatively and I asked how she happened to select this particular dog. She said, "That was easy but it almost didn't happen."

Still grieving over the loss of a much loved dog of her own some years before, she had not planned on getting another dog, but one spring day as the puppies played in the front yard she stopped and petted the romping group and felt strongly drawn to this particular dog. Taking a liking to him she visited regularly. Over several days she felt a special bond with this little pup. After much encouragement from her neighbor to select one of the dogs, she finally decided to give a home to this special dog, only to be told that he had been promised to another family. Doris went home that night and somehow felt a great sense of loss, reporting that she cried off and on all night.

To her surprise, her neighbor called her the next day saying, "Somehow I just didn't feel right about him going to that other family, we want you to have him." Doris was ecstatic; still pinching herself and saying, ". . . but I wasn't planning on adding a dog to our family." She could hardly wait to pick him up!

To make a long story short, Doris found herself in a whole new world, the world of therapy animals. Brady was a natural and seemed to have this special sense of how to be present with people who would respond to his kind of sensitivity and affection. She went on to tell me several very touching stories of times and places where she had gone into, hospitals, nursing homes and homes for children and adults with special needs; the boy with cerebral palsy who hadn't spoken in weeks and when Brady was about to leave he put his arm around him and said, to the staffs amazement, "I love you." Brady was always the star, winning the hearts of those with whom he came in contact.

Another touching story was an unplanned encounter. Doris related that, "Brady goes with her everywhere." As she came into the bank one day, Brady seemed to be on a mission. He immediately pulled in the direction of a lady standing in line with others at the window. Brady nuzzled the hand of a lady standing alone and then leaned gently against her, looking up into her eyes. Immediately the woman began to cry. With big tears running down her face she explained to Doris, "Just two days ago my dog of 15 years had to be put to sleep and I have been devastated at the loss. You can't know how much this means to me that you and this special dog have come over to me, it brings me great comfort. Thank you!"

By this time I was standing there with tears in my eyes. I thanked her for sharing the stories and for sharing Brady's nuzzle with me. Doris exclaimed, "God has given me a very special ministry that I never expected to have and I'm so thankful." Soon, Doris and Brady went on down the street. As I wiped away my tears, my spirit too felt lifted. I couldn't have agreed more with her assessment of a gift from God.

Prior to this encounter I hadn't thought of God bringing comfort through the winsome ways of a dog, but perhaps he does. In the bible we read, "Blessed be the God and Father of our Lord Jesus Christ, the Father of mercies and the God of all consolation. He comforts us in all our sorrows so that we can comfort others in their sorrows with the consolation we ourselves have received from God."(2 Corinthians 1:3,4, alt.)

Rob Kronberg, Chaplain, 4/27/06
The Samarkand Retirement Community
Santa Barbara, CA.
The article was written for the bi-weekly
news letter, "The Sam News."

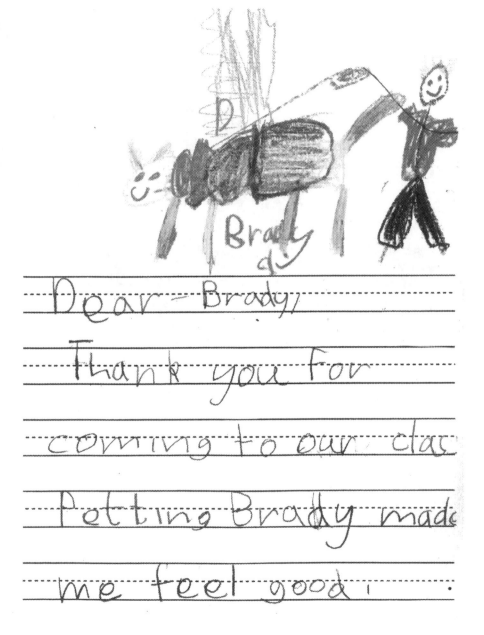

Dear Brady,

Thank you for

coming to our clas

Petting Brady made

me feel good.

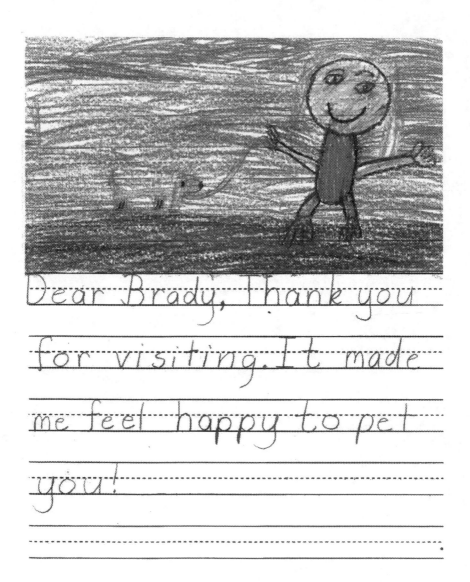

Dear Brady, Thank you for visiting. It made me feel happy to pet you!

Dear Brady,

Thank you for coming

to my classroom. I like

the tricks, they were fantastic

Mon, May 20, 2002

Dear Mrs. Doris Clancy & "Brady,"

Thank you for coming to our class. I really enjoyed listening about your work. Brady was really friend I bet he makes the patience feel a lot better. I know when I was in the hospital, there were dogs that came around to visit. They made me feel good, because they reminded me of my pets at home.

Brady was a real treat, and I got to sit next to him in the picture. Thank you again for coming

P.S. Brady's tricks were great!

About the Author

Our journey began eleven years ago when a little puppy melted my heart, and I realized we were able to communicate through thought. He was a natural at being a therapy pet which led to many adventures. I learned why people were so drawn to Brady, his ability to know who needed him the most, and that he had a sense of humor. I started to write our memoirs because I needed to heal my soul after he died, to remember all he gave to so many, to honor his life and smile, and not to mourn his death and cry. My husband, Gary, and I live in beautiful Santa Barbara, California, with Samantha cat, and someday, when the time is right, we will adopt another dog to join our family.